YOU CHOOSE
BOOKS ™

The CHILD LABOR
Reform Movement

An Interactive History Adventure

by Steven Otfinoski

Consultant:
Jeffrey Newman
President/Executive Director
National Child Labor Committee
New York

CAPSTONE PRESS
a capstone imprint

You Choose Books are published by Capstone Press,
1710 Roe Crest Drive, North Mankato, Minnesota 56003.
www.capstonepub.com

Library of Congress Cataloging-in-Publication Data
Otfinoski, Steven.
  The child labor reform movement : an interactive history adventure / by Steven
Otfinoski.
      pages cm.— (You choose. History)
  Includes bibliographical references and index.
  Summary: "Describes the history of child labor and reform from three different
perspectives"—Provided by publisher.
  Audience: Grade 4 to 6.
  ISBN 978-1-4765-0255-7 (library binding)
  ISBN 978-1-4765-3608-8 (paperback)
1. Child labor—History—Juvenile literature. 2. Child labor—Law and
legislation—Juvenile literature. I. Title.
  HD6231.O84 2014
  331.3'109—dc23   2013007023

Editorial Credits
Adrian Vigliano, editor; Bobbie Nuytten, designer; Wanda Winch, media researcher;
Charmaine Whitman, production specialist

Photo Credits
AP Images/North Wind Picture Archives, 26; The Bridgeman Art Library/UIG/
Universal History Archive, 22; Getty Images/George Eastman House/Lewis
W. Hine, 62, Hulton Archive, 37; Library of Congress: Prints and Photographs
Division, 42, 59, 101, 102, Lewis Wickes Hine, cover, 6, 10, 49, 56, 67, 74, 81, 86,
91, 92; Mary Evans Picture Library: Illustrated London News Ltd., 31; North Wind
Picture Archives, 12; SuperStock Inc./Image Asset Management Ltd., 21

Printed in the United States of America in Stevens Point, Wisconsin.
032013   007227WZF13

TABLE OF CONTENTS

ABOUT YOUR ADVENTURE

YOU live in the world of the Industrial Revolution. New machines produce things in great numbers and create new demand for goods. Factories are built in cities. Men and women are hired to operate the factory machines. Children are hired too.

In this book you'll explore how choices meant the difference between life and death. The events and work you'll experience happened to real people.

Chapter One sets the scene. Then you choose which path to read. Follow the directions at the bottom of each page. The choices you make will change your outcome. After you finish one path, go back and read the others for new perspectives and more adventures.

YOU CHOOSE the path you take through history.

The spinning room of a cotton mill in 1911 was a crowded, dangerous place.

A Revolution Begins

Before the Industrial Revolution, clothing and other goods were mostly made by people in their homes or in workshops. Work was done by hand or with simple machines. By the mid-1700s in England, inventors created new power-driven machines. These machines could make many more goods than workers could by hand. The machines were put in factories.

Workers came to cities to work in factories. They didn't make a lot of money, but it was more than they could earn on farms and in workshops.

Turn the page.

The Industrial Revolution quickly spread from England to other countries in Europe. It also spread to North America. Every industrialized country grew in population and wealth.

But the Industrial Revolution also brought new problems. The factory workers were not paid well. They worked 12 to 14 hours a day, six days a week. Working conditions in factories were often dirty and unsafe.

It was not only adults who put up with industrial work. Children worked to help with their family's income. Employers liked to hire children because they would work for less money than adults. Children were less likely to complain about low pay or bad working conditions. They were also small enough to do jobs in tight spaces.

Some child workers were only 5 or 6 years old. Child workers often weren't allowed to attend school. They were exposed to pollution and machines that could injure or even kill them in an accident. Men called overlookers punished children who worked too slowly.

Social reformers such as Jacob Riis and Lewis W. Hine and nonprofit organizations such as the National Child Labor Committee spread the word about the hardships of child labor. People were shocked by the reformers' photographs and newspaper stories. Laws restricting child labor began to be passed in Great Britain, Germany, and later, the United States. But many of these laws weren't passed until the late 1800s and early 1900s.

Turn the page.

Social reformer Lewis Hine photographed a girl working in a Georgia cotton mill in 1909.

You are a child living during the Industrial Revolution and its aftermath. Like thousands of other children, you must work to survive or help your family. All of the available jobs are hard and possibly dangerous. Which job will you choose?

❧ To be a boy working in a cotton mill in England, turn to page **13**.

❧ To be a girl working in New Bedford, Massachusetts, turn to page **43**.

❧ To be a "newsie" selling newspapers in New York City, turn to page **75**.

Smoke from England's factories filled the air during the Industrial Revolution.

CHAPTER 2

The Pauper Apprentice

It is summer 1799 in England. Your country is in the midst of a time of great change called the Industrial Revolution. Yet there is no change in your life as an 8-year-old orphan boy in a workhouse near the city of Nottingham. You work each day crushing animal bones to be used in fertilizer. It is hard work, but the workhouse officials feed and clothe you. The food isn't great, but you aren't starving.

You also attend school in the workhouse. The classes are noisy and disorganized, but you put up with it because you want to learn to read and write.

Turn the page.

Then one day in August, a man comes to the workhouse. His name is John Merton. You and about 80 other children march into the big hall to hear him speak. You and your friend Freddy wonder what this is all about. Freddy is also 8, but he's much smaller than you.

Mr. Merton stands at the front of the room. "You lucky children have been chosen to come with me to Lowdham Mill to become pauper apprentices."

You have heard of Lowdham Mill, where cotton is turned into cloth. You're not sure what a pauper apprentice is, but it sounds important. Mr. Merton says you will eat roast beef and plum pudding every day. You will be well paid for your work and learn to be ladies and gentlemen. On your days off, you will ride the masters' horses.

You and the other children are excited. Lowdham Mill sounds like heaven compared to life at the workhouse.

Mr. Merton says you can leave for Lowdham Mill that day if you sign a contract. You and Freddy rush to join the line of children. Finally you find yourself at the head of the line, where Mr. Merton is sitting at a desk.

"Sign here, lad," he says. You scan the contract on the table before you. Unlike many of the children, you are a good reader. The contract says that you must remain a pauper apprentice until you are 21. That seems like a very long time. Mr. Merton said nothing about how long you would have to work at the mill. If he left out that detail, are the other things he said true?

➤ To sign the contact, turn to page **16**.

➤ To not sign, turn to page **30**.

15

You sign the contract. Freddy signs one too. "Good lads," says Mr. Merton. "Get your things, and then find a place in the wagon out in front."

The two of you grab your few possessions. The wagon is old and shabby, and you are crowded inside with all the other children. But you don't mind.

You arrive at the mill late in the day. You go to the dining hall, where you're given a plate of boiled potatoes. "Where's the roast beef?" you ask the cook. She just laughs.

After supper you go to the apprentices' lodging. It is a dirty, broken-down building. Your room is crowded with 30 beds. Two boys share each bed. The room is cold and unheated. But you're so tired that you hardly notice.

The next morning you are awakened very early. The overlooker, James Frank, takes you to the mill.

The mill is an amazing place with long lines of spindles with cotton thread. Men and women sit at machines that spin the cotton threads into cloth. Mr. Frank explains that you can choose between two jobs. Most of the smaller boys, like Freddy, are scavengers. They pick the loose cotton from under the machines. But because you are tall for your age, you can be a piecer. You'll repair the broken threads on the machines.

17

→ To be a scavenger, turn to page **18**.

→ To be a piecer, turn to page **23**.

You're a bit tall for a scavenger, but by becoming one you can stay with the boys your own age. Freddy is working in the same part of the mill. Your job is to crawl under the machines and pluck out the loose cotton strands from the machinery. If left there the cotton would jam the machine.

The air is filled with dust, oil, and cotton floss, making it difficult to breathe. Your back aches from all the bending and crawling. But the worst part of the job is the danger. The machines are running at full speed as you crawl under each one. Move too close to the whirling gears and you could lose a hand or an arm—or even your life.

One day after another lunch of boiled potatoes, Freddy looks across at you with fearful eyes. "I can't do this anymore," he tells you in a shaky voice. "I can't stand the noise, and the machines scare me."

You wish you could tell Freddy to take a break and rest on the floor for 15 minutes. But you just had lunch. There will be no break until the whistle blows at 6 p.m.

There is a way you can help Freddy. You can do his work for a while. But if the overlooker catches you, he will beat both of you.

➤ To help Freddy, turn to page **20**.

➤ To go on with your own work, turn to page **36**.

"I'll take care of your work for a while," you whisper to Freddy, "but look busy. The overlooker is nearby."

Freddy smiles at you gratefully. You crawl under his machine and start pulling out the cotton strands.

About 10 minutes later you hear a shout. It is Mr. Frank, the overlooker. You turn and see Freddy. He's curled up on the floor with his eyes closed.

"What's this?" says Mr. Frank. "Resting on the company's time?"

He hits Freddy on the back with his billy club. Freddy screams in pain. Mr. Frank strikes him again.

Crawling beneath the machines in a cotton mill was dangerous work.

"Don't hit him!" you yell.

"Stay out of this," hisses Mr. Frank, "or you'll get a beating too!"

✦ To mind your own business, turn to page 22.

✦ To help Freddy, turn to page 33.

The overlooker beats Freddy for several minutes as you watch helplessly. Then he turns to you.

"Tried to help your friend by doing his work for him, did you?" he says. "I'll see that doesn't happen again. Go see Mr. Merton across the floor. Lad, you've just joined the ranks of the piecers."

Illustration from an 1840 novel by Frances Trollope that explored the plight of child workers

Being a piecer has some advantages over scavenging. You don't have to crawl under the machines. There's less chance of being injured. But the work is just as hard. You repair broken threads on the spinning machines. You lean on the machine and tie the threads back together. You are no sooner done with one repair than another spinner calls for your help.

You'd give anything to be able to rest for even a few minutes. Catherine Lewis, a spinner with a kind face, calls you over.

"You look tired," she says quietly. "It's rough on your first day, isn't it?"

You nod, grateful that someone understands.

Turn the page.

"There's a small room in the back where we girls go when we want a little peace at lunchtime. You can go there and rest for a few minutes."

You thank her, but she sees the hesitation in your eyes.

"Don't worry," she tells you, "I'll see that none of the others give you away to the overlooker. But don't be gone too long."

➤ *To keep working, go to page **25**.*

➤ *To take a rest in the back, turn to page **32**.*

You walk to the iron tank, which holds water. You splash water on your face. That will help keep you awake.

You are walking back to your post when Mr. Merton enters with two men and a woman. You can't hear what they're saying over the noise of the machines. Then to your surprise, the group approaches you.

"What is your job here, young man?" asks the woman.

"He's a piecer, Mrs. Hillman," says Mr. Merton.

Mary Hillman looks at him sharply. "I asked the boy, Mr. Merton, not you."

You can see that she and her two friends don't like Merton. You wonder what they are doing here.

"How old are you, boy?" asks one of the men.

Turn the page.

"Eight," you reply.

"And do you like it here?" asks the man. "Do you want to stay?"

Merton is glaring at you. Say how you really feel, and you'll be in trouble. But if you tell the truth, could it make a difference?

A government inspector checks on young factory workers.

→To lie and please Merton, go to page **27**.

→To tell the truth, turn to page **34**.

"I'm happy enough," you murmur.

The visitors look at you with doubt. "Are you sure?" says Mrs. Hillman. "Do not fear this man."

But you do fear him. "I'm fine," you insist.

Mrs. Hillman turns away from you. "Very well," she says. "We will leave. But we shall return."

They walk out the door. Mr. Merton pats you on the shoulder. "Good lad," he says.

"Who are they?" you ask.

Mr. Merton spits, "Reformers. Now back to work, boy."

That night you lay in bed, unable to sleep. The idea of working in the mill for the next 13 years weighs on you. You could run away. But if you're caught, you will face a horrible punishment.

→ To run away, turn to page **28**.

→ To stay, turn to page **38**.

If you're going to run away, night is the best time to do it. You wrap your few possessions in a cloth and tiptoe across the darkened room past the sleeping boys. A guard sits outside the door, but he is asleep too.

You start to walk down the road leading into town. It is about 6 miles, but you don't stop to rest. You know by morning Merton will be hunting for you.

It is nearly dawn when you reach the town. You walk the streets, your stomach aching with hunger. Suddenly a man with a black mustache stops you. He stares at your dirty clothes and haggard face. "Just come into town, lad?" he asks you. You nod. "I'll bet you could use a good meal."

You could, but you don't know if you can trust this stranger.

"I'm looking for a clever boy to work for me," he says.

"What kind of work?" you ask.

"Come with me for a meal and I'll tell you about it," says the man.

→ To go with the man, turn to page **39**.

→ To keep moving, turn to page **40**.

You hand the pen back to Mr. Merton. "I can't sign this contract, sir," you tell him.

"Why not?" asks Mr. Merton.

"I'm sorry," you say, "but I don't trust you."

Mr. Merton gives you an angry look. "Next!" he cries.

Freddy looks stunned. You want to tell him not to sign. But the man shoos you away. As you leave the hall, you see Freddy sign the contract. Have you just made a huge mistake?

About a week later, a tattered letter arrives for you from Freddy. He says that Lowdham Mill is not at all what Mr. Merton promised it'd be. The work is harder than at the workhouse, and the food and lodging are miserable.

You feel bad for Freddy, but relieved at the same time. You continue to work and attend school at the workhouse. One day you will leave here with a good education, ready to start a new life.

The system of English workhouses lasted into the 1900s.

THE END

To follow another path, turn to page 11.
To read the conclusion, turn to page 103.

You find a spot on the floor of the back room. You plan to rest only a few minutes, but soon you are asleep. You are dreaming about eating roast beef when the overlooker, Mr. Frank, awakens you.

"I'll teach you to sleep on the job!" he cries, lifting you by the back of your neck. He carries you over to an iron holding tank for water. He dunks you headfirst into the tank. You squirm at the shock of the cold water. Mr. Frank's grip on your legs slips, and you fall into the tank. You hit your head on the hard bottom and drown before Mr. Frank can pull you out. It's a horrible end to your first day in the mill.

32

THE END

To follow another path, turn to page 11.
To read the conclusion, turn to page 103.

"Leave him alone!" you cry.

Mr. Frank continues to whack poor Freddy with his club. You manage to grab the club and pull it from his grip. Mr. Frank is shocked more by your daring than your strength. He cries out for help.

Three big overlookers run to you. They pin you to the floor and hit you. You try to defend yourself, but there are too many fists coming at you. After about a minute, they lift you to your feet and push you back to your workplace.

The next day you and Freddy are sent back to the workhouse. After the mill the workhouse seems like a safe, kind place.

33

THE END

To follow another path, turn to page 11.
To read the conclusion, turn to page 103.

"No, I don't like it here, and I don't want to stay," you say.

"The lad's a troublemaker," says Mr. Merton quickly. "Don't believe a word he says."

Mrs. Hillman bends down and takes your hand in hers. "Go on, lad," she says. "You needn't fear this man."

You tell the visitors about the false promises Mr. Merton made. When you finish the man turns to Merton. "Sir, we have heard enough. If half of what this boy says is true, this mill should be shut down and you and your employers put on trial."

"They're all lies!" cries Mr. Merton.

"We will see," says Mrs. Hillman. "In the meantime this boy is coming with us."

Mr. Merton's face turns a deep red. "What?" he exclaims. "You can't do that. He's signed a contract!"

"We will buy out his contract," she says sharply. "Take us to your manager."

The two men nod. Mr. Merton sputters but says nothing.

Mrs. Hillman takes your hand. Together you walk out of the mill. A new life is just beginning for you.

THE END

To follow another path, turn to page 11.
To read the conclusion, turn to page 103.

You can't help Freddy. It'll only get you both into more trouble.

"You can do it," you say, putting your arm around his shoulder. Freddy nods and wipes the tears from his eyes. You crawl back under the machine and try to keep an eye on Freddy. You look away for a moment and hear Freddy scream. Blood is spurting from his right hand. It is caught in the gears of the machine. You pull at his legs with both hands. You manage to free him, but his hand is torn off completely. You yell for help, and two overlookers rush to your side. They lift Freddy and take him away.

Later that afternoon you learn that Freddy died of blood loss and shock. If you had only taken his place for a while and let him rest, he might still be alive.

Some mill workers were too poor to afford protective clothing such as shoes.

THE END

To follow another path, turn to page 11.
To read the conclusion, turn to page 103.

You roll over and try to sleep. It's too soon to think of running away. And anyway, you need to come up with an escape plan. But as the days march on, you give up the idea. You are too tired at the end of each long workday to even think about it.

Your main hope is to survive the conditions of the mill until you turn 21 and are free to live your life as you choose. That is the one thought that keeps you going.

THE END

To follow another path, turn to page 11.
To read the conclusion, turn to page 103.

The stranger takes you to a shop where you eat your fill of meat pies.

"Now about that job," says the man. "Have you ever picked pockets before, lad?"

So that's it. He's a crook and wants to put you on his crew. Well, it's better to be a pickpocket than a beggar.

"No," you tell him, "but I'm willing to learn."

The man laughs. "Good lad," he says. "We'll start your education at once."

And so you enter a life of crime. You think you can quit whenever you want, but it doesn't work that way. In a year you have moved on to armed robbery. You're afraid you will either end up in a jail cell or hanging from a noose.

THE END

To follow another path, turn to page 11.
To read the conclusion, turn to page 103.

You turn down the man's offer. You're starving, but you don't like this stranger's shifty eyes. You go from shop to shop looking for work. But no one will hire you. You decide to try begging. You join other boys in an alleyway. You lay out your handkerchief and call out to the passers-by for a coin or two.

"Poor lad," a woman says. You hear a clink of coins on your handkerchief. The voice sounds familiar.

You look up and see the surprised face of Mrs. Hillman, the kind lady from the mill. "What are you doing here?" she asks.

You tell her how you ran away and how you wish you'd been honest with her earlier. She looks at you for a long moment and says, "Come, son. I'm taking you home with me. We're going to get you off the street and see you start a new life."

A new life. You can hardly believe your ears. You take her hand and walk from the dark alley into the bright light of day.

THE END

To follow another path, turn to page 11.
To read the conclusion, turn to page 103.

As the long journey from Europe ended, passengers waited for their first glimpse of New York.

CHAPTER 3

Factory Girl

It is spring 1906. Your family has just arrived in the United States from Italy. You left because your family's farm failed, and your father couldn't find work. You, your parents, and your seven brothers and sisters traveled across the Atlantic on a big, crowded ship.

Once in New York, you travel north to the town of New Bedford, Massachusetts. You have relatives and friends from Italy there. New Bedford is an exciting place with many stores and a seafront filled with fishing boats. But life here is not as easy as you expected.

43

Turn the page.

In New Bedford food and housing are expensive. Everyone in your family who is old enough must work. Your father and older brothers get jobs in a factory. Your mother goes to work in a cloth mill.

You are 10 years old and must work too. Your Aunt Sophia tells you about three businesses that are hiring in New Bedford. One is a seafood cannery. Another is a laundry. The third place is a glove factory.

➻ To work in the cannery, go to page **45**.

➻ To work in the laundry, turn to page **48**.

➻ To work in the glove factory, turn to page **50**.

You'll give the cannery a try. The foreman, Edward Willis, inspects your hands. They are hardened by years of working on the farm in Italy. "Good hands for shucking," he says. "Come on, I'll give you a tour."

You follow him into the cannery, wondering what shucking is all about.

"The oysters have to be shucked before they get canned," Mr. Willis explains. "That's what girls your age do here. You remove the oysters from their shells."

The first thing you notice is the smell. It's a wet, fishy smell that fills the place and everything in it. You hold your nose.

Turn the page.

Mr. Willis introduces you to a young woman. "This is Mrs. Elizabeth Riley," he says. "She'll show you what to do."

Mrs. Riley shows you how to shuck an oyster. She stands at a metal counter and lifts an oyster from a pile. She takes a small knife in her other hand and slips the blade into the thin space between the two shells. With a twist of the knife, the oyster pops open. She slices out the meat, dumps it into a pail, and then sweeps the shells onto the floor.

"It's not hard to pry them open," explains Mrs. Riley. "They cook them a bit before we get them. It relaxes them."

You go to work alongside Mrs. Riley. The oyster shells are hard and bumpy. Soon your fingers are raw and bleeding from handling them. The oyster juice stings the cuts on your hand.

Mr. Willis comes by just before your lunch break. "How's it going?" he asks.

You would like to quit right now and find another job. But it's possible the other jobs have already been filled. What will you do?

➻ To quit and apply at the laundry, turn to page **48**.

➻ To stay at the cannery, turn to page **51**.

The next morning you go to the laundry to apply for work.

"Any experience in a laundry?" asks Sam Randall, the big man sitting behind the office desk.

"I help my mother with it at home," you say.

Mr. Randall laughs. "What we do here is a bit different. But we'll give you a try."

He leads you into the laundry room. The air is thick with steam from the machines. In minutes your body is coated with sweat. The windows are all nailed shut to keep out dirt from the street. The steam and strong chemical odor make breathing difficult.

Girls are washing the clothes in large vats. Others are squeezing water from the clothes by pushing them through a metal press called a mangle. A third group is ironing the cleaned clothes.

"You can work with the mangle or do the ironing," Mr. Randall says.

Immigrant workers often lived in crowded, noisy tenement buildings.

➤ To work with the mangle, turn to page **53**.

➤ To work with the ironing, turn to page **59**.

The glove factory consists of many large rooms. There are long tables with sewing machines in each room. A female operator sits at each machine, sewing together pieces of the gloves.

As the foreman leads you to your table, you are surprised to hear the girls singing.

"Welcome," says a blond girl sitting across from you. "I'm Blanche."

You tell her your name. "Why were you singing?" you ask.

Blanche laughs. "We sing to make the time pass, and it helps keep us working at a steady rhythm."

50

Operators are paid only for the work they produce. The goal is to make 12 pairs of gloves in an hour—one pair every five minutes.

→ *Turn to page* **54.**

"It's fine," you say. But the tears in your eyes give you away.

"Not tough enough for the shucking?" Mr. Willis asks.

"Why don't you put her with the kiddies?" asks Mrs. Riley.

"She's a little old for a sitter," he replies. "But we could use another girl with them today. That Annie ain't much good."

You're not sure what they're talking about.

"Well, girl," says Mr. Willis, "are you willing to babysit with the workers' kiddies?"

You've babysat for years with your younger brothers and sisters. It's better than having your hands cut by oyster shells. You follow Mr. Willis.

Turn the page.

Outside about eight children ages 2 to 4 are playing near a railroad car full of shellfish. One girl, who looks about 7, is rocking a baby in her arms.

"Annie, this is a new girl who will be helping you," says Mr. Willis to the girl with the baby. He then walks back to the factory.

"Thank goodness," says Annie. She hands the baby to you. "I'm not good with babies."

You think you're good with babies, but this one cries and cries. You rock her faster.

Meanwhile, two little boys start throwing oyster shells at each other. Annie tries to stop them, but they push her away. She turns to you for help.

The baby is still crying. Should you give her to Annie so you can attend to the boys?

➻ To stay with the baby, turn to page **64**.

➻ To stop the fight, turn to page **66**.

The mangle is a nasty-looking piece of equipment, consisting of heated rollers that squeeze excess water from the wet clothes. It's hot, wet work.

You throw a batch of wet clothes onto the mangle. A bracelet on your wrist gets caught in the clothes and comes off. Your grandmother gave you the bracelet before you left Italy. It will be crushed if it goes through the mangle. You realize that you shouldn't have worn it to work. Can you snatch it back without getting mangled yourself?

53

➤ To snatch the bracelet off the mangle, turn to page **58**.

➤ To let the bracelet go, turn to page **69**.

After several hours of work, it is time for lunch. As you eat Blanche talks in a low voice.

"We operators aren't happy," she tells you. "We have to pay the management 50 cents a week for the power to run our sewing machines. We even have to buy our own needles and pay for the oil that runs the machines. And we only earn $3 a week. It's not right."

"But what can we do about it?" you ask.

"The men in the glove cutters' department have formed a union. Some of us girls are thinking about joining it. A union would help us fight for our rights. Would you like to come to the union meeting tonight?"

➤ *To go to the union meeting, go to page 55.*
➤ *To turn down the invitation, turn to page 57.*

Most of the people at the meeting are men from the glove cutters' department. You sit in the back with the small group of women. The men argue about what they should do.

"There's only one way the bosses are going to listen to us, and that's to go on strike," says a young man.

"And lose our jobs?" cries out an older man. "We'll be cutting our own throats!"

Many men agree with this. Then Blanche rises to her feet.

"We won't lose our jobs," she says boldly. "They can't operate this factory without us. I say we strike! It's the only way to make things better."

Turn the page.

You wish you were as courageous as Blanche is. The issue of the strike is not settled that night. But you sign up for the union along with Blanche and the other women.

Glove workers often worked long hours in crowded spaces.

↠*Turn to page* **70.**

You tell Blanche you can't go to the meeting because you told your parents you'd be home early.

"Well, maybe next time," Blanche says.

Both of you return to work. A thin man carrying a large camera walks into the factory. He introduces himself as Lewis Hine, a fire inspector. "I'll have to take some pictures to show what the building looks like inside," he says. "Do you mind if I take your pictures too?"

Some of the girls don't want to be in Hine's picture, but you think it will be fun. No one has ever taken your picture before.

→ *Turn to page 61.*

You can't lose your grandmother's bracelet! You reach out your hand and grab the bracelet just before the rollers seize the clothes and begin to press. If you'd been a few seconds slower, your hand or even your entire arm would have been crushed.

"That was foolish," a woman named Millie working nearby tells you.

"I know, but I couldn't lose that bracelet," you reply.

Just then Mr. Randall comes by. "You shouldn't have a girl that young on the mangle, Mr. Randall," says Millie ."She's bound to have an accident."

"Maybe you're right," he says. "We'll move her to ironing."

The ironing in the laundry is done by a big machine, which you operate with your hands and feet. The machine consists of two giant sets of gas-fueled rollers. The bottom roller acts as an ironing board and the top roller as the iron, pressing down on the clothes.

Laundry workers had to be careful because they operated heavy, dangerous machinery.

Turn the page.

After an hour your feet and hands are sore from the work. But there will be no break until lunch. Suddenly you smell something odd. Something's burning!

Another girl stares in horror at one of the ironing machines. "Look!" she cries. "Fire!"

The heat from the iron rollers has set some clothes on fire. The flames are spreading quickly. The girls race toward the front entrance. They fight to get through the small door. You notice a rear door that no one is trying to get through. It could be your way out.

➤ To wait your turn out the front door, turn to page **65**.

➤ To try the rear door, turn to page **68**.

"You can take my picture," you tell Mr. Hine. He tells you to hold still at your machine. When he is done, he calls you over and asks you to stand in front of him.

You notice that Mr. Hine wears a vest with many buttons down the front. He glances down at the top of your head and writes something down on his notepad. He says, "Button number four," to himself as he writes. Then he asks for your name and address so he can send you a copy of the photo. After you give him your information, he beckons you to come closer.

"You see, my name is Lewis Hine, but I'm not really a fire inspector. I'm a professional photographer. I took your picture for the National Child Labor Committee."

"What's that?" you ask him.

Turn the page.

"It's an organization that opposes how child labor is done in this country and wants better regulation. The photographs I take show the public the evils of child labor and expose it for what it is. I hope you don't mind."

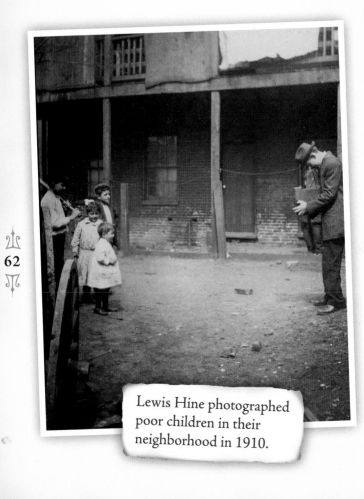

Lewis Hine photographed poor children in their neighborhood in 1910.

"I don't, as long as I don't get into trouble," you tell Mr. Hine. "What did you mean by button number four?"

"Well, I can't always talk to children and find out how old they are," he replies. "So I see which button they come up to on my vest. That tells me how tall they are—and then I can usually figure out how old they are. But I'd better leave before the foreman comes and starts asking questions," he says, walking away.

"What did he say to you?" Blanche asks when you return to the sewing table.

→ To tell Blanche who Hine really is, turn to page 72.

→ To keep Hine's identity a secret, turn to page 73.

You sing to the baby, and she falls asleep. The two boys throw shells at Annie.

"Stop that!" you cry. You're bigger than Annie, and they listen to you.

"What's going on here?" says Mr. Willis, entering the area.

"I can't take anymore. I quit!" says Annie.

Mr. Willis notices the sleeping baby. "How did you manage that?" he asks you.

"I have a way with babies," you reply.

"Well, you're the new full-time babysitter then," he says. "You'll stay with the children every day. Does that suit you?"

You smile. "It suits me fine, sir," you tell him.

THE END

To follow another path, turn to page 11.
To read the conclusion, turn to page 103.

You join the line for the front door. One small girl is pushed to the floor. You lift her to her feet before the others trample over her in their panic. You both squeeze through the door as the flames quickly spread.

Everyone stands outside and watches as the fire devours the laundry. Orange flames shoot up into the blue midday sky.

"Well," says Olive, the girl whose life you saved, "it looks like we're all out of a job now."

You know Olive's right. But at least you got out with your lives. Tomorrow is soon enough to worry about the next job.

THE END

To follow another path, turn to page 11.
To read the conclusion, turn to page 103.

You hand the baby to Annie and rush to the fighting boys. One stops and goes back to the other children. The other boy throws a shell that hits you in the eye. Then he turns and runs. Angry, you run after him.

The boy leads you around and around the railroad car. After several minutes, you manage to grab him and haul him back to the group.

To your surprise, a woman is now holding the baby. Mr. Willis is standing next to Annie. His face is red with anger. "Did you leave Annie alone with the baby?" he asks you.

"Just for a moment," you begin, but the woman cuts you off.

"Annie dropped my little Maggie on the ground!" she snaps.

"It was an accident," Annie protests.

Young workers shucked oysters and babysat.

"Quiet, girl," snaps Mr. Willis. Turning to you, he says, "You're the older one. You shouldn't have left her alone with that baby. Get your pay for the hours you've been here. You're fired."

You have to go home with only a few pennies to show for your day. You hope you will find another job tomorrow.

THE END

To follow another path, turn to page 11.
To read the conclusion, turn to page 103.

You run to the rear door. You twist the doorknob. It turns, but the door won't open. You yank hard on the doorknob, again and again. The door won't budge. You turn to go back to the front door. But a wall of flames has spread across the room, cutting you off from the front door. There is no way out. Too late you realize there was a reason no one else was going for the rear door. This mistake will cost you your life.

THE END

To follow another path, turn to page 11.
To read the conclusion, turn to page 103.

The bracelet isn't worth risking your life. You listen to the crushing sound as the bracelet slides under the rollers.

Suddenly the mangle comes to a grinding halt. Some of the other girls turn and stare at you coldly. Mr. Randall runs over to see why the mangle is stopped.

"It was her," says one girl, pointing at you. "She let something through the mangle that shouldn't have been there."

"I'm sorry," you begin, but Mr. Randall isn't listening. He fires you for causing the machine to break down. You don't know how you'll explain this to your parents. They'll be so disappointed that you lost your job the first day.

THE END

To follow another path, turn to page 11.
To read the conclusion, turn to page 103.

The following Monday the union is put to its first test. One of the glove cutters has been fired unfairly. The other glove cutters walk off the job. You and Blanche tell your fellow operators you should do the same. They agree.

At 3 p.m. you rise from your tables and walk toward the door.

"Where are you going?" asks the foreman, Robert Olson.

"We're leaving to support the union," you tell him.

Mr. Olson laughs. "There's nothing to support," he says. "The man who was let go has been rehired. So get back to work."

The others start to go back, but you stop them. "Wait," you say. "We'll go back. But not until you stop charging us for needles, oil, and the power for the sewing machines."

Mr. Olson stares at you, his mouth open. "Go back to work," he says again.

"We won't until we get what we asked for," says Blanche. "We have the union behind us."

Mr. Olson looks uncertain. "You're all crazy," he finally says. "But I'll talk to the manager and see what he says."

"And we'll wait here until you come back," you tell him.

Blanche hugs you. "I think we've won this battle," she says. "Thanks for speaking up."

"Thanks for giving me the courage to do it," you reply.

THE END

To follow another path, turn to page 11.
To read the conclusion, turn to page 103.

71

"He's a photographer here to take pictures of us girls," you whisper to Blanche.

"What did you say?" she asks you, cupping her hand to her ear.

"He works for a group that wants to help child workers," you tell her a little too loudly.

You notice two other girls at the next table nod at one another. Did they hear what you said?

When your workday ends, the foreman calls you into his office. "I heard about the photographer who took your picture," he says. "He won't be coming back here again. Neither will you, little lady."

How will you explain this to your parents? You know Lewis Hine is doing good work, but you wish you had kept quiet.

THE END

To follow another path, turn to page 11.
To read the conclusion, turn to page 103.

"He was just getting my name and address," you tell Blanche.

A few days later when you come home from the factory, you find a large envelope waiting for you. You open the envelope and find a photo of yourself at your sewing machine. There is a note from Mr. Hine thanking you for supporting the right to improve rights for child workers. Maybe this will change things as much as the union would. You hope so.

THE END

To follow another path, turn to page 11.
To read the conclusion, turn to page 103.

Lewis Hine photographed a poor young boy and his family in their New York City home.

CHAPTER 4

Newsies On Strike

It is 5 a.m. July 20, 1899, in Lower Manhattan, New York City. You wake up in the room you share with your brother. Because it's summer, there is no school. But you still have a long day ahead of you. You are a "newsie," a boy who sells newspapers on the streets. You buy newspapers from the publishers and then sell them for a small profit.

You hear your father coughing in the other room. He's been sick for a long time. He needs medicine from the drug store. It costs a dollar. That's a lot of money. You're determined to earn that and more today selling papers.

75

Turn the page.

You head into the street with your news bag on your shoulder. You walk toward the offices of the *New York Journal,* one of the city's most popular morning papers. Other newsies wait by the circulation manager's window.

A short boy with an eye patch approaches. You recognize him as Kid Blink. He is a well-known newsie.

"Don't you fellows know you shouldn't be here?" Kid Blink tells them. "Today's the day the strike against the *Journal* starts."

One boy glares at Kid Blink. "Forget your strike," he says. "I've got to sell papers to help my family."

"Sure, but you don't have to sell Hearst's paper. Not after what he's done to us," says Kid Blink. William Randolph Hearst is the wealthy publisher of the *Journal*. "The *Journal* and the *New York World* have raised the wholesale price we pay from 50 cents to 60 cents for 100 papers," explains the Kid. "He doesn't raise the prices for his customers, but he doesn't mind robbing us newsies of another dime."

You like Kid Blink, and maybe his strike is a good idea. But you need to sell those papers. Your father's health depends on it.

Just then the circulation manager's window snaps open. "Please don't," Kid Blink says to you as you head for the window. "We've got to stick together. It's the only way to get the price down."

→ To join the strike, turn to page **78**.

→ To buy the papers, turn to page **80**.

If you help with the strike against the *Journal* and the *World* in the morning, you can buy copies of the afternoon papers later. They haven't raised their prices, and you aren't striking against them.

Kid Blink claps you on the back. "Come on, pal, we've got to meet up with some friends."

As you walk he tells you you're going to meet the other strikers at the office of the *New York World*. The *World's* publisher, Joseph Pulitzer, has also raised his wholesale price.

In a few minutes you arrive at the *World* offices. About 20 newsies greet you.

"What's the plan, Kid?" pipes up Al, a small boy who looks to be no more than 7.

"The delivery wagons are lined up," Kid Blink says. "We've got to stop them from making their paper deliveries to the newsstands and shops."

You and the other boys pick up small stones from the street and hurl them at the horse-drawn wagons as they approach. One angry wagon driver leaps from his seat. He grabs Al and begins to drag him toward the wagon. Kid Blink is trying to keep the other boys together, but many of them are running away. Maybe you'd be wise to join them.

→ *To help Al, turn to page* **81**.

→ *To run away, turn to page* **94**.

"How many papers?" the man in the window asks you.

"I'll take 150," you say, trying to sound confident.

Kid Blink turns away in disgust. The man at the window whistles.

"That's a lot of papers to sell in one day," he says. He's right—and what you don't sell you can't return.

"I'll sell them," you say.

"That'll be 90 cents," the man says.

It's every cent you have. If you sell each paper for 2 cents, you will make $3. At least $2 of that will be profit—enough for you to buy medicine for your dad.

→ *Turn to page* **83**.

You toss a stone at the driver who grabbed Al, hitting him in the arm. He lets go of Al and charges at you. You dodge his attack and run after Al.

New York newsies waiting to pick up papers at the *World*.

Turn the page.

When the two of you are a few blocks away, you stop to catch your breath.

"Thanks, pal," says Al with a smile.

"Don't mention it," you say. "Well, I guess we better catch up with Kid Blink and see what he wants us to do next."

Al shakes his head. "Sorry, but I can't waste any more time on the strike," he says. "I've got to earn some money today. Otherwise my dad will be really mad."

You think of your own dad, lying sick in bed. The afternoon papers will be going to press in a few hours. You won't be defying the strike to sell them.

→ To join up with Al, turn to page **85**.

→ To return to the strikers, turn to page **100**.

It's 6 a.m. now, and the streets are filled with people rushing to work. "Paper! Get your *New York Journal*," you cry.

A man stops and buys a paper from you. Then you sell another. You put the pennies in your pocket. You'll use them later to make change if someone gives you a nickel or dime.

You see a corner with no newsie on it. This is surprising. Most of the good corners are taken by older newsies who claim them as their territory. You decide to take this corner for yourself.

In 10 minutes you have sold nearly 30 papers. Then you hear a gruff voice. "What do you think you're doing here?"

Turn the page.

You turn to face a husky boy, at least several years older than yourself. "This is my corner," he said. "Now beat it, you punk."

"But I was here first," you say.

The boy leans down. "I said beat it, before I beat you into a pulp."

⇢ *To flee the scene, turn to page **86**.*

⇢ *To stay and fight, turn to page **95**.*

You stick with Al. You have a few hours before the afternoon papers will be off the presses. The two of you stop to buy lunch from a street vendor.

An hour later you are standing outside the circulation office of the *New York Post*. There is a long line of newsies ahead of you. Finally you reach the head of the line.

"I'll take 100," you say. You ought to be able to sell that many before nightfall. Selling the papers at 2 cents each, you'll make a profit of $1.50. And maybe more with tips. Al takes 100 too.

"Maybe we should split up," says Al.

That might be a good idea. You could probably do better on your own.

→*Turn to page* 89.

You decide not to risk a fight. You are about half a block away when a well-dressed man calls out to you. He is standing in the doorway of a saloon. From the way the man slurs his words, you know he's been drinking.

Newsies learned to deal with all sorts of people as they sold papers around the city.

"I saw what that bully did to you," he says. "I feel sorry for you. Gimme 10 of those papers."

"You want 10?" you say with surprise.

"Yeah," replies the man. "I'll give one to each of my buddies when they come in for a drink." He hands you a bright silver half-dollar.

You are about to say you don't have enough change for a half-dollar, but then you remember that the man is drunk. Maybe if you give him 5 cents—change for a quarter—he won't notice. You know it's wrong to cheat, but you need money for your father's medicine.

→ To cheat the customer, turn to page 88.

→ To return his half-dollar, turn to page 96.

You take the half-dollar and give the man back change for a quarter. He stares dumbly at the coins in his palm. "Hey, you gave me the wrong change," he says slowly.

You could say you made a mistake, but you panic. You turn and run.

"Thief! Stop, thief!" cries the man.

Unluckily for you a police officer is passing by. He sees you running and blows his whistle. "Stop!" he cries. But you don't.

Another cop joins in the chase. You run around a corner and see an alley on your left. Next to the alley is a fire escape leading to the roof of a building.

→ *To climb the fire escape, turn to page* **93**.

→ *To duck into the alley, turn to page* **97**.

You wish Al good luck and strike off for Battery Park at the end of Lower Manhattan. You sell a few papers along the way. Battery Park is crowded, but you don't sell many papers.

The afternoon drags into evening. You're hungry, but you can't go home until you've sold all your papers. You pass a restaurant filled with people. You might be able to sell your remaining papers in there. But some restaurant owners don't like newsies bothering their customers.

➻ To enter the restaurant, turn to page **90**.

➻ To stay on the street, turn to page **99**.

You enter the restaurant and move from table to table. Several people buy your papers. A waiter frowns at you but says nothing. Just then a young man sitting at a corner table calls out to you.

"Say kid," he says in a low voice. "How would you like to sell all those papers and get a bonus of a dollar on top of it?"

You catch your breath. "Sure," you say.

He pushes a small package wrapped in brown paper across the table. "I need someone to deliver this package to an address in the Bowery neighborhood. Do it, and the money's yours. When you get there, knock twice on the door and ask for Ed. Give the package only to Ed. Do you understand?"

You don't know what's in the package, but you're pretty sure this man is up to no good. Is the money worth possibly getting into trouble with the law?

Newsies sold papers throughout New York City.

→ To turn down this offer, turn to page **92**.

→ To take the package, turn to page **98**.

You shake your head at the man. "I don't think that's a good idea," you tell him.

He grabs your arm. "Get out of here, then," he says as shoves you out the door.

There were newsies of many different ages, and not all of them were boys.

➤ *Turn to page* **99.**

You rush up the fire escape and see both policemen passing below. They never look up to see you.

You feel a twinge of guilt about not joining the strikers. If you didn't have to pay so much for the Hearst and Pulitzer papers, you wouldn't be so desperate to sell your papers. Maybe you wouldn't have even considered cheating the gentleman. It's time you join your friends on the picket line. You jump across a few rooftops and climb down another fire escape.

93

→ *Turn to page* **100**.

You follow the other boys who are running away. You slip and fall.

"Watch out!" someone cries. You look up and see a wagon pulled by a runaway horse. It's heading straight at you! The wagon's wheel runs over your right foot. You scream in pain. Several people gather around you.

"Someone get a doctor!" one man cries. An ambulance comes, and two men load you into it. Your foot is too mangled to save and must be amputated. Your newsie days are not over, however. People feel sorry for boys with missing limbs and body parts. They usually get good sales and lots of tips. But what a price to pay for a successful career as a newsie.

THE END

To follow another path, turn to page 11.
To read the conclusion, turn to page 103.

"It's my corner now," you say.

The big guy gives you a mean grin. "You asked for it, punk."

He pushes you to the ground and punches your face with his fists. You taste blood in your mouth. He finally gets off you.

"Now beat it," he says.

Several newsies watching the fight are laughing. You turn to get your papers, but they're gone. Someone stole them while you were fighting. Now you have to go home empty-handed. You don't know how you're going to break the bad news to your parents.

95

THE END

To follow another path, turn to page 11.
To read the conclusion, turn to page 103.

"Sorry," you say, "but I don't have change for this." You hand the man back his half-dollar.

The man takes it and fishes a shiny quarter and a dime from his pocket. "Here, kid," he says, handing you the coins. "I like your honesty. Keep the change."

A 15-cent tip! That's the biggest of the day. You thank him and continue to sell your papers. Within two hours you have sold your last paper. Now you can buy the medicine and head home for dinner. It's been a great day.

96

THE END

To follow another path, turn to page 11.
To read the conclusion, turn to page 103.

You dash up the alley and hide in the shadows. One policeman runs by, but the other one stops and peers into the darkness. You step back into the alley. The cop enters and starts moving toward you. You panic and run. You come to a brick wall. There's no escape.

"All right, son," says the cop. "I'm taking you in for petty theft."

You are bound for the stationhouse where you will be charged. The police will contact your parents. This has turned into the worst day of your life.

THE END

To follow another path, turn to page 11.
To read the conclusion, turn to page 103.

You take the package.

You hurry to address in the Bowery. You knock twice. The door opens on a dark room.

"I have a package for Ed," you say.

A man steps into the light of the street lamp. He wears a badge. He's an undercover police officer! He takes the package and grabs your wrist. "Ed's downtown at the police station. You'd better go there with me too. I've got some questions for you."

You pull away and run. He doesn't come after you. You're not worth the time to chase.

You get the medicine and then head home. This was an exciting day, but it could have ended with you in jail. You'll know better than to do something like that again.

THE END

To follow another path, turn to page 11.
To read the conclusion, turn to page 103.

Back on the street, it's getting late. You pass a hospital. The door opens, and a young man steps out. "Paper, please," he says.

You pull one out of your bag. The man pays you and studies the front page. "July 20, 1899. A day to go down in history."

You look puzzled. The man laughs. "My wife just had our first baby," he explains. "And that makes today very special. How many papers do you have?"

You count them. "Thirty-five," you reply.

"I'll take them," he says. "I want everyone I know to have the paper from the day my son was born."

You gratefully take the money. Coming down to Lower Manhattan wasn't such a bad idea after all.

THE END

To follow another path, turn to page 11.
To read the conclusion, turn to page 103.

You catch up with the other striking newsies. Kid Blink claps you on the shoulder. "We're going to Union Square," he says. "We're going to rally and show everyone that we're united against Hearst and Pulitzer."

The rally is a success, with hundreds of newsies turning out. The other newspapers cover the rally. News of the strike spreads.

By August 2 both Hearst and Pulitzer realize the strike is hurting their business too much. They agree to a compromise. They won't roll back the wholesale price to the newsies, but they will refund the price of any unsold papers. For many newsies, that is as good, if not better, than lowering the wholesale price.

New Yorkers parade in protest against child labor in the early 1900s.

The next day you and the rest of the newsies are back at work. You'll never forget those two weeks in 1899 when the newsies took on two of the most powerful men in New York and came up winners.

THE END

To follow another path, turn to page 11.
To read the conclusion, turn to page 103.

Jacob Riis wrote about the working conditions of the young and poor.

CHAPTER 5

The End of Child Labor

Child labor was an accepted fact of life for centuries in Europe and the United States. But by the early 1800s, people in England and the United States were speaking out against it. In 1832 English politician Michael Sadler introduced a bill in Parliament to outlaw children younger than 9 from working. It failed to pass, but a similar bill passed in 1847.

In the United States, in 1836 Massachusetts passed a law requiring working children younger than 15 to attend school at least three months a year. In 1842 Massachusetts was the first state to limit children's working hours to 10 each day.

103

But child labor continued to spread. By 1870 about 750,000 children were working in the United States. Thirty years later that number had more than doubled. About 1.7 million children ages 10 to 16 were employed, along with 250,000 children younger than 10.

Reporters such as Jacob Riis wrote about the evils of child labor. His book *How the Other Half Lives*, published in 1890, opened the eyes of Americans to the horrors of child labor.

In 1906 photojournalist Lewis Hine began taking photos of child workers for the newly established National Child Labor Committee. The committee was dedicated to reforming and restricting child labor in the United States. Hine would pretend to be a fire inspector, insurance salesman, or Bible salesman to get into mills and factories to take pictures of child workers.

In 1912 the government created the U.S. Children's Bureau to represent the rights of children in the workplace. In 1916 Congress passed a national child labor law. But two years later, the U.S. Supreme Court declared the law unconstitutional.

Another 20 years would pass before a national child labor law was passed in 1938 as part of the Fair Labor Standards Act. But child labor has not been entirely erased. Some children, many of them the sons and daughters of recent immigrants, continue to labor in migrant farmwork and in factories and other workplaces.

Across the globe the picture is much worse. According to a report from the International Labor Organization, about 246 million children between the ages of 7 and 15 work worldwide. The struggle to end child labor in the world has a long way to go.

TIMELINE

1750s—Power-driven machines in England and Scotland revolutionize the textile industry and begin the Industrial Revolution.

1789—English textile worker Samuel Slater comes to the United States and later builds the first water-powered textile mill.

1814—Francis Cabot Lowell establishes a textile factory in Waltham, Massachusetts, and hires young farm girls as workers.

1830s—Industrialization spreads quickly throughout the eastern United States and employs many children.

1842—Massachusetts passes a law limiting work hours for child workers.

1870—The U.S. Census records child laborers for the first time.

1890—Photojournalist and social crusader Jacob Riis publishes his book *How the Other Half Lives*, an exposé of poverty in American cities and the abuses of child labor.

July 1899—Newsboys in New York City and surrounding areas go on strike against two newspapers that have raised their wholesale prices; the strike ends two weeks later with a compromise from the publishers.

1900—The U.S. Census records that 18.2 percent of all children from ages 10 to 15 are working.

1906—A national law against child labor fails to pass in Congress.

The National Child Labor Committee is founded in the United States; Lewis Hine goes into factories and mines to take photos of child workers.

1912—President William Howard Taft creates the Children's Bureau to oversee the needs of American children.

1916—Congress passes the National Child Labor Act to restrict child labor in the United States.

1918—The U.S. Supreme Court declares the National Child Labor Act unconstitutional.

1938—The Fair Labor Standards Act finally puts an end to much of the legal child labor in the United States.

1941—The U.S. Supreme Court rules that the Fair Labor Standards Act is constitutional; the U.S. has a lasting law that limits child labor.

OTHER PATHS TO EXPLORE

In this book you've seen how the events surrounding child labor look different from several points of view.

Perspectives on history are as varied as the people who lived it. You can explore other paths on your own to learn more about what happened. Seeing history from many points of view is an important part of understanding it.

+ Compare your life with the life of a child during the Industrial Revolution. How is it similar? How is it different? Use details from the text to support your answer. (Key Ideas and Details)

+ Reformers in the United States worked hard to expose the problems of child labor. Even with the public attention, decades went by before the government passed a law banning child labor. What were some reasons people resisted the end of child labor? Do you think their resistance was valid? Explain why or why not. (Integration of Knowledge and Ideas)

+ While the majority of newsies participated in the strike against Hearst and Pulitzer's newspapers, some didn't. These newsies faced attacks by the striking newsies. What motivated them to keep working? Suppose you were one of the newsies. Would you have participated in the strike or continued to work? Explain your reasons. (Integration of Knowledge and Ideas)

READ MORE

Avi. *City of Orphans.* New York: Atheneum Books for Young Readers, 2011.

Burgan, Michael. *The Breaker Boys: How a Photograph Helped End Child Labor.* Mankato, Minn.: Compass Point Books, 2012.

Robinson, J. Dennis. *Striking Back: The Fight to End Child Labor Exploitation.* Mankato, Minn.: Compass Point Books, 2010.

Scott, Janine. *Kids Have Rights Too!* New York: Children's Press, 2008.

INTERNET SITES

Use FactHound to find Internet sites related to this book. All of the sites on FactHound have been researched by our staff.

Here's all you do:
Visit *www.facthound.com*
Type in this code: 9781476502557

GLOSSARY

apprentice (uh-PREN-tuhs)—someone who learns a trade or craft by working with a skilled person

cannery (CAN-uh-ree)—a factory where seafood or other food is canned

foreman (FOR-muhn)—a person in charge of a group of workers

mangle (MANG-guhl)—a metal machine that presses excess water from washed clothes in a laundry

newsie (NOOZ-ee)—a child who sold newspapers on the streets in the late 1800s and early 1900s; most newsies were boys

pauper (PAW-pur)—a very poor person who lives on charity or welfare

reformer (re-FORM-uhr)—someone who works to improve something in society

revolution (rev-uh-LOO-shun)—an uprising by a group of people against a system of government or a way of life

scavenger (SKAV-uhn-jer)—a mill worker who plucked loose strings from machines

union (YOON-yuhn)—an organized group of workers that tries to gain better pay and working conditions for workers

wholesale (HOLE-sayl)—sale of goods in quantity to retailers who sell to the public

workhouse (work-HOWS)—a place where poor children and adults lived and worked

BIBLIOGRAPHY

Baldwin, Peter C. *Domesticating the Street: The Reform of Public Space in Hartford, 1850–1930.* Columbus: Ohio State University Press, 1999.

Herndon, Ruth Wallis, and John E. Murray, ed. *Children Bound to Labor: The Pauper Apprentice System in Early America.* Ithaca, N.Y.: Cornell University Press, 2009.

Hindman, Hugh D. *Child Labor: An American History.* Armonk, N.Y.: M.E. Sharpe, 2002.

Kirby, Peter. *Child Labour in Britain, 1750–1870.* New York: Palgrave Macmillan, 2003.

Levine, Marvin J. *Children for Hire: The Perils of Child Labor in the United States.* Westport, Conn.: Praeger, 2003.

INDEX